Dip Me In Color

An Abstract Coloring Book

Book 2

Written & Illustrated By: Tanya Cochran

ISBN-13:
978-0-9979413-0-2

DEDICATION

This book is dedicated to Teenagers all over the world!

(Hugs)

CONTENTS

What is this book all about?

This is an abstract coloring book. It's the second book in the Dip Me In Color book series. **50** more drawings that are even more crazy and wild than the first book.

I prefer abstract and unusual. It helps me tap into my quirky creative side. I like to draw pages of things that might remind you of something else, but that have no real existence. They are interesting and super fun to color. Psychologists have said that the more abstract a coloring page is, the more benefits it has. The colorist is free to use whatever color he/she chooses and can color it however they like!

Coloring has been doing so much for our mental well-being. How can it help you? Studies show that it can reduce stress and anxiety, help with focusing and fine motor skills, and help tap into your creative side. These are just to name a few. You can look up a great November 2015 article with the Huffington Post on coloring…very interesting!

On the opposing side of the drawings are scriptures taken from the bible. I hope they will inspire and encourage! I've gotten a lot of great feedback via email and Facebook! I've been encouraged by all the great messages! Thank you!

The content in these books are all abstract, but all are appropriate for all ages.

Please feel free to visit my website as periodically I add other fun items that coincide with the books!

www.dipmeincolor.com

Let the stresses of life go away for a little while. ☺ Hopefully you have already experienced this from book 1! Enjoy the series!

You can add in your own fun and creativity with color! I would love to hear from you! tanyacochran@mail.com

ACKNOWLEDGMENTS

A special thank you to all of you who have embraced the weirdness in me. For loving all my art projects. Thank you to those of you who have validated me as a human being. We all need that. I'm so blessed by the awesome people in my life! Especially my husband and kiddos!

Thank you to all my family and friends that I love so sooooo much!

And thank you for the Bible…God's Holy word. I'm inspired by the promises that I have placed in this book. I used a few different versions of the bible for the scriptures in the book including the New King James Version, New Living Translation, and the New International Version.

And most importantly I thank my Lord and Savior Jesus for my life and for blessing me greatly! Nothing is possible without you Lord!!!

Page B

Psalm 23:4

Yea, though I walk through the valley of the shadow of death, I will fear no evil: for thou art with me; thy rod and thy staff they comfort me.

Psalm 89:11

The heavens are thine, the earth also is thine: as for the world and the fullness thereof, thou hast founded them.

Matthew 7:7
Ask, and it shall be given you; seek, and
ye shall find; knock, and it shall be
opened unto you.

Psalm 16:8
I have set the LORD always before me:
because he is at my right hand, I shall
not be moved.

1 Corinthians 13:13
And now abideth faith, hope, charity, these three; but the greatest of these is charity.

Psalm 46:10
Be still, and know that I am God: I will
be exalted among the heathen, I will be
exalted in the earth.

Proverbs 3:5-6

Trust in the LORD with all thine heart; and lean not unto thine own understanding. [6] In all thy ways acknowledge him, and he shall direct thy paths.

Isaiah 40:31
But they that wait upon the LORD shall renew their strength; they shall mount up with wings as eagles; they shall run, and not be weary; and they shall walk, and not faint.

John 8:32
And ye shall know the truth, and the truth shall make you free.

Philippians 1:6
Being confident of this very thing, that he which hath begun a good work in you will perform it until the day of Jesus Christ.

Matthew 25:40

And the King shall answer and say unto them, Verily I say unto you, Inasmuch as ye have done it unto one of the least of these my brethren, ye have done it unto me.

Psalm 19:14
Let the words of my mouth, and the
meditation of my heart, be acceptable in thy
sight, O LORD, my strength, and my
redeemer.

John 16:33

These things I have spoken unto you, that in me ye might have peace. In the world ye shall have tribulation: but be of good cheer; I have overcome the world.

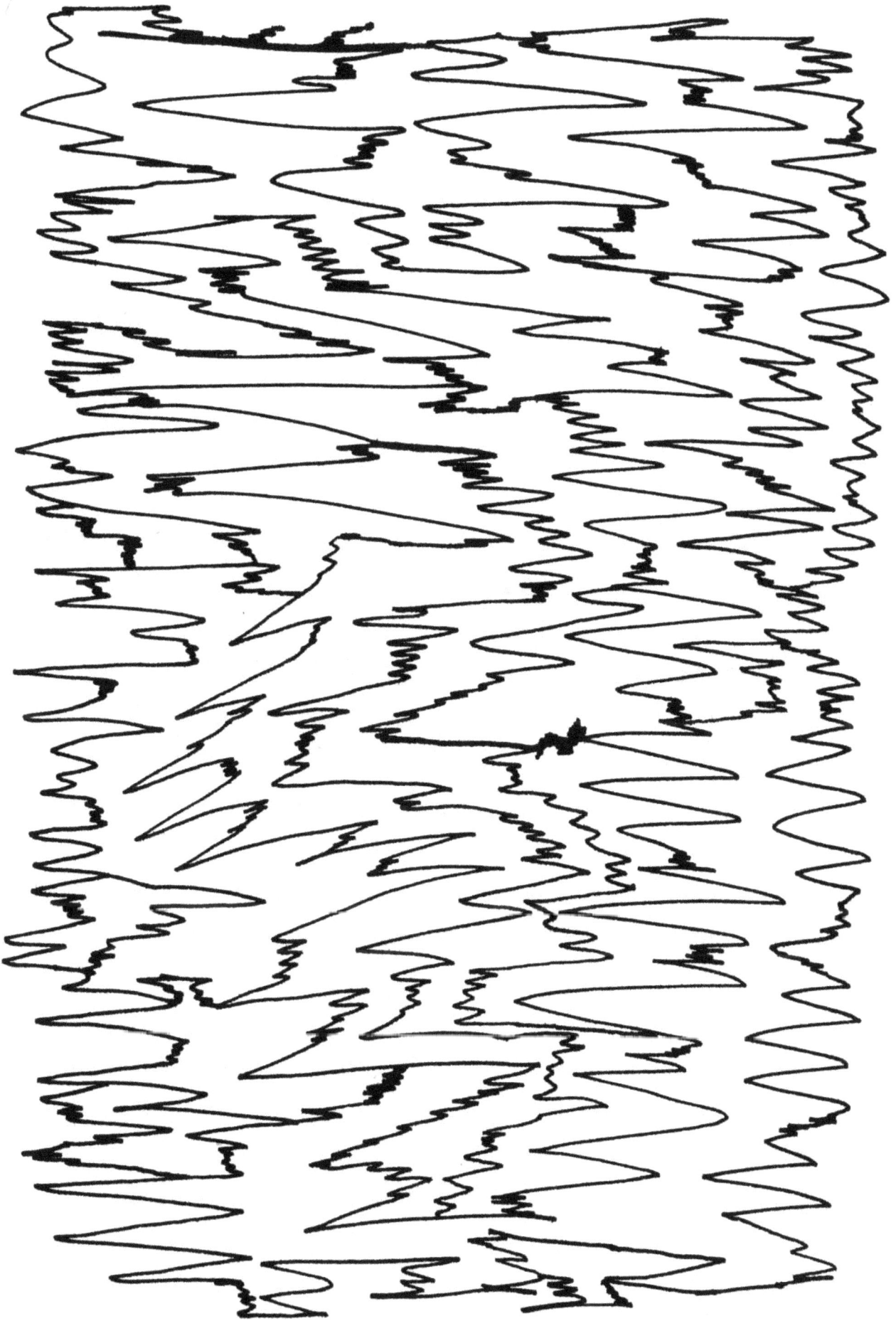

2 Timothy 2:7
Consider what I say; and the Lord give thee
understanding in all things.

Matthew 11:28-30

Come unto me, all ye that labor and are heavy laden, and I will give you rest.

Take my yoke upon you, and learn of me; for I am meek and lowly in heart: and ye shall find rest unto your souls.

For my yoke is easy, and my burden is light.

Matthew 6:19-21

Lay not up for yourselves treasures upon earth,
where moth and rust doth corrupt, and where
thieves break through and steal:
But lay up for yourselves treasures in heaven,
where neither moth nor rust doth corrupt, and
where thieves do not break through nor steal:
For where your treasure is, there will your
heart be also.

Psalm 88:2

Let my prayer come before thee: incline thine ear unto my cry:

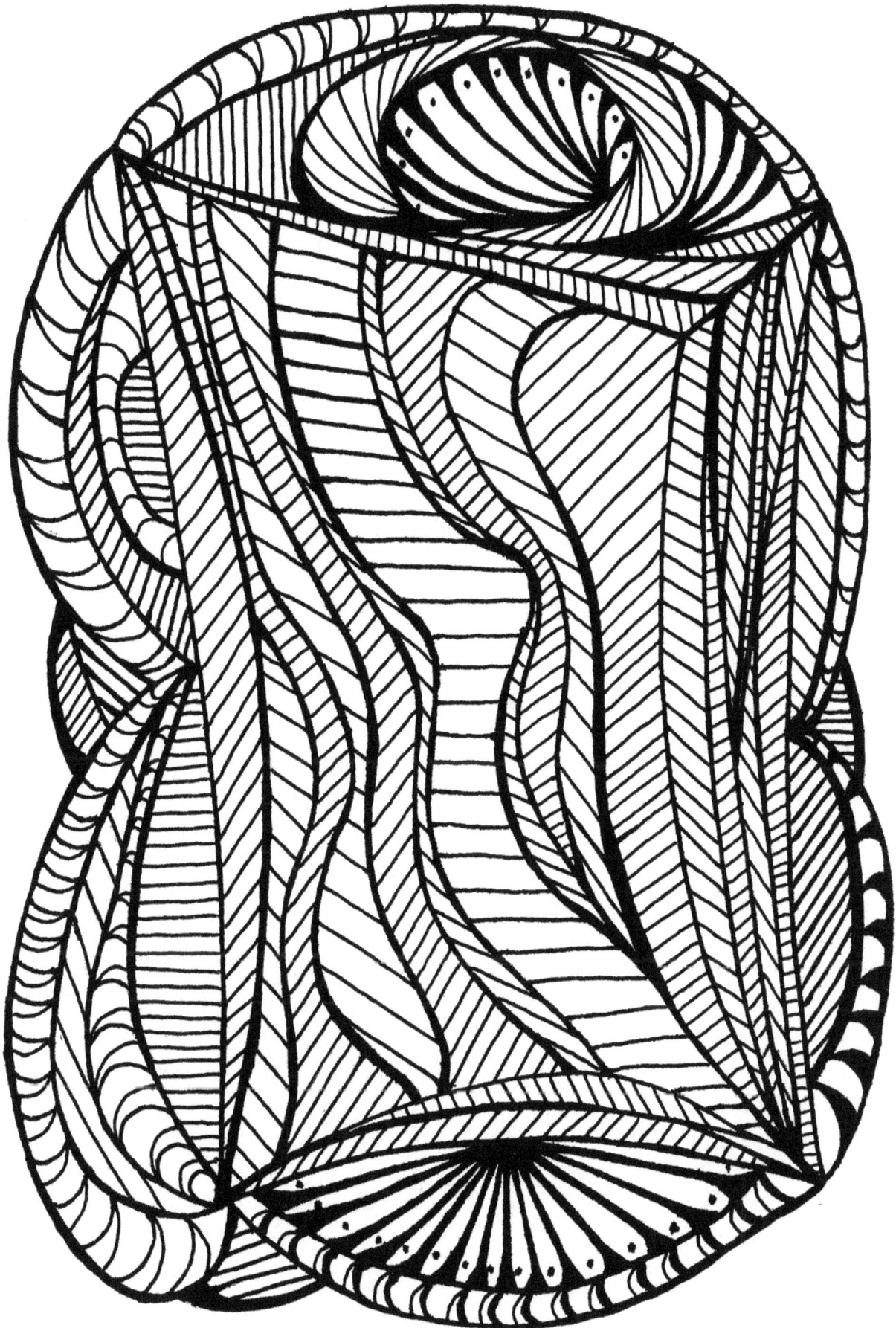

1 John 3:18
My little children, let us not love in word,
neither in tongue; but in deed and in
truth.

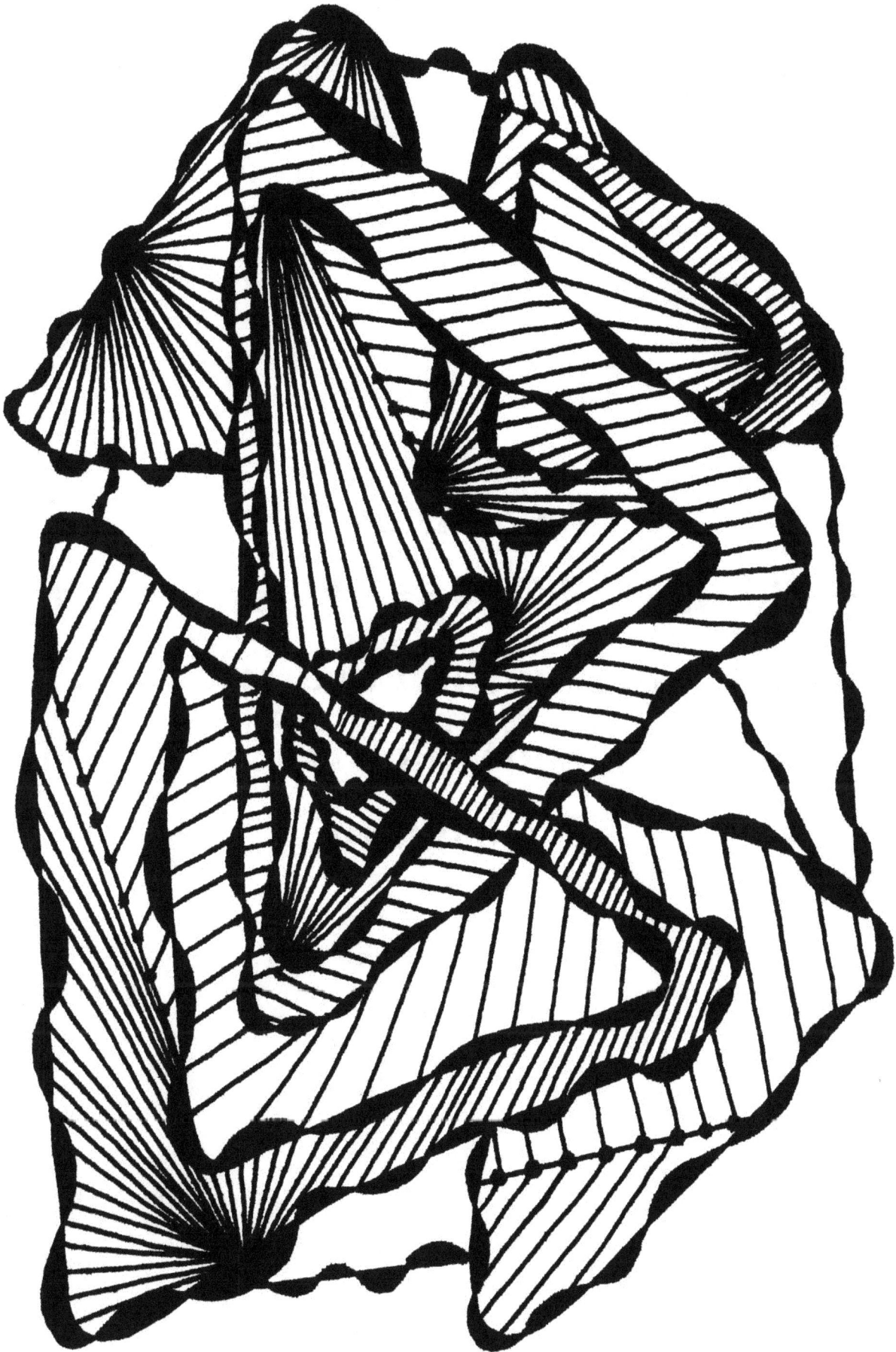

Revelation 1:8
I am Alpha and Omega, the beginning and the ending, says the Lord, which is, and which was, and which is to come, the Almighty.

Proverbs 30:5
Every word of God is pure: he is a shield unto them that put their trust in him.

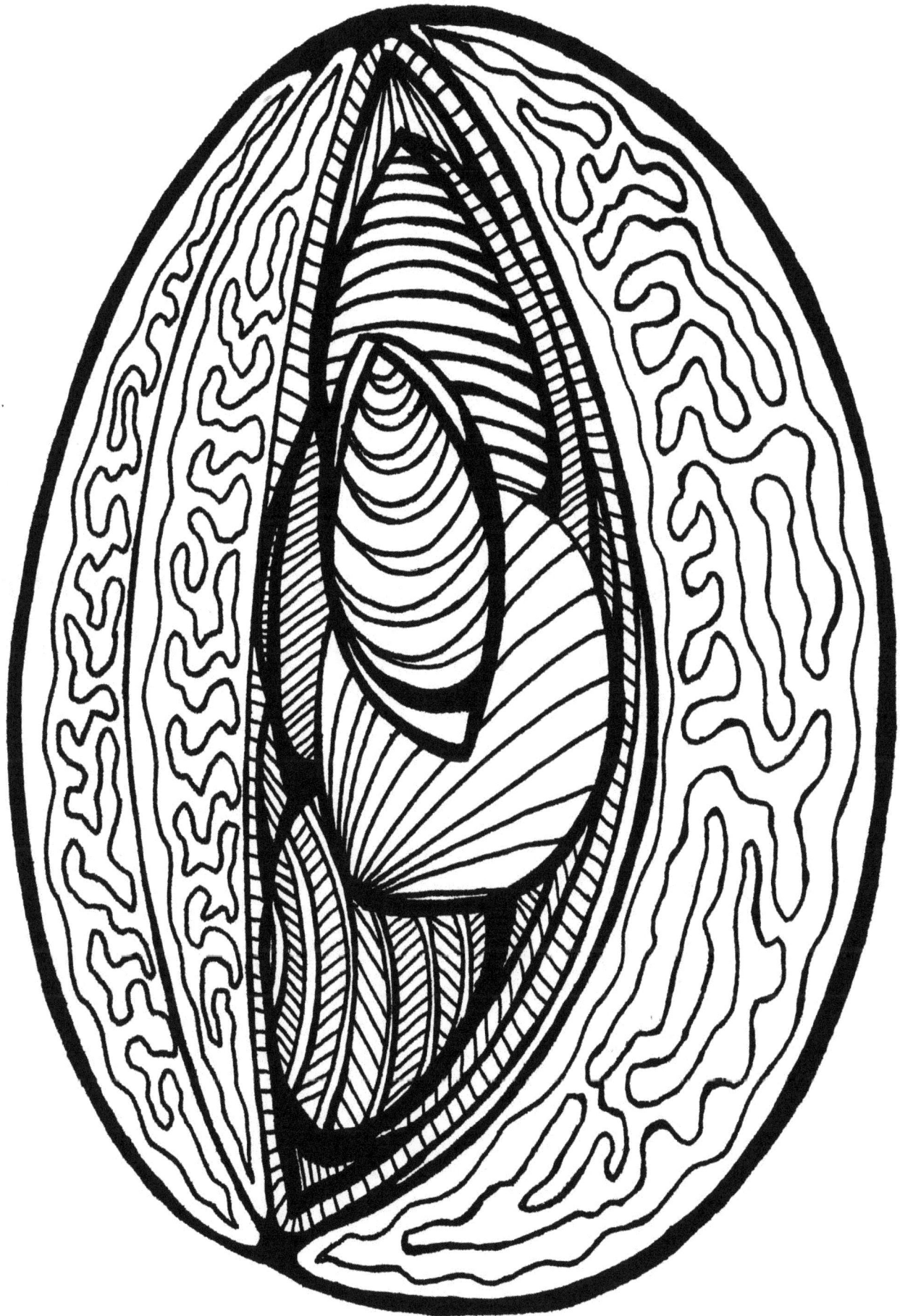

Psalm 119:11

Thy word have I hid in mine heart, that I might not sin against thee.

Psalm 31:24

Be of good courage, and he shall strengthen your heart, all ye that hope in the Lord.

Jeremiah 33:3
Call unto me, and I will answer thee, and show thee great and mighty things, which thou knowest not.

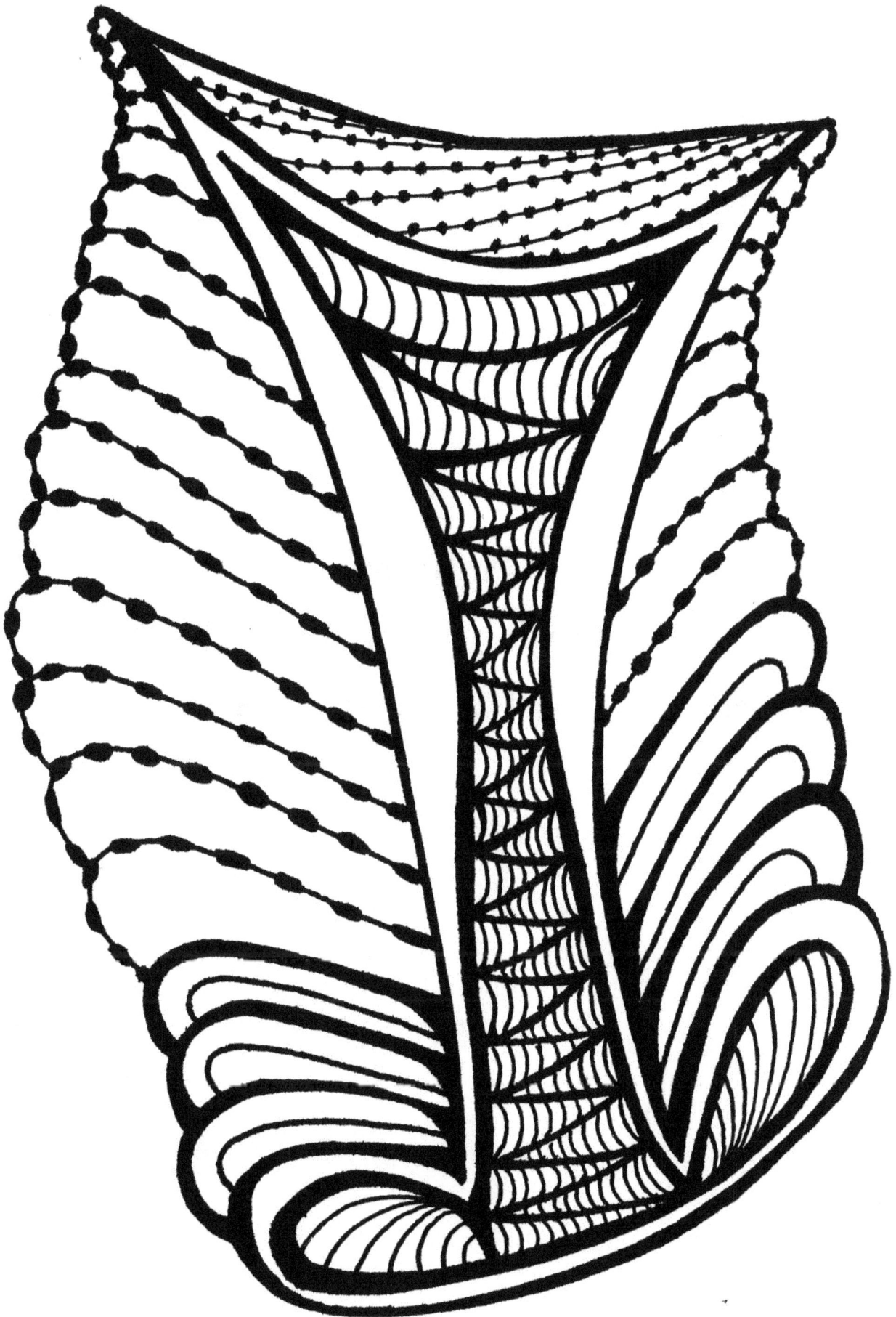

Nahum 1:7

The Lord is good, a strong hold in the day of trouble; and he knoweth them that trust in him.

Psalm 145:21
My mouth shall speak the praise of the Lord:
and let all flesh bless his holy name for ever and
ever.

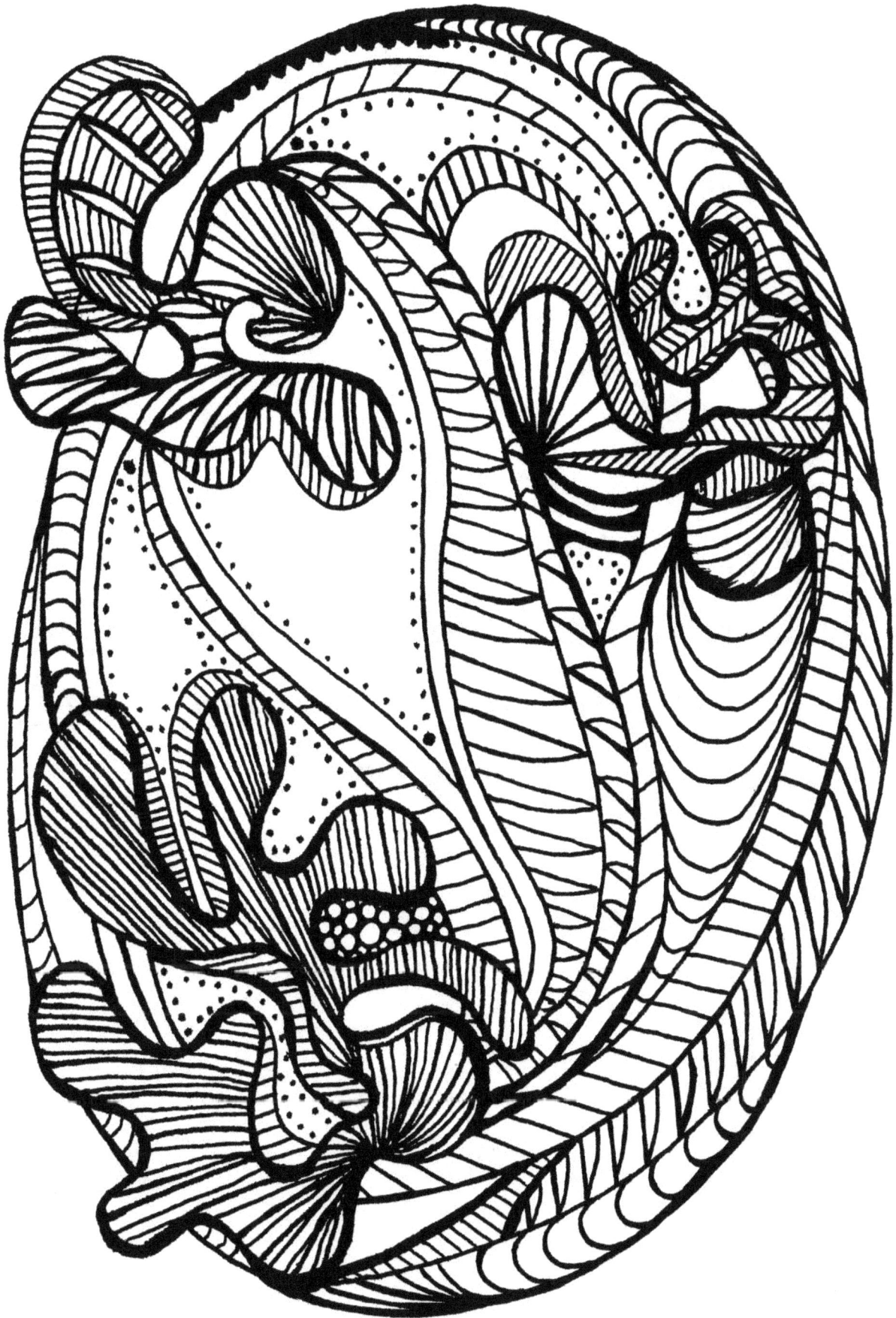

Micah 6:8

He hath shewed thee, O man, what is good; and what doth the Lord require of thee, but to do justly, and to love mercy, and to walk humbly with thy God?

Jeremiah 32:27
Behold, I am the Lord, the God of all flesh: is there anything too hard for me?

Isaiah 55:12

For ye shall go out with joy, and be led forth with peace: the mountains and the hills shall break forth before you into singing, and all the trees of the field shall clap their hands.

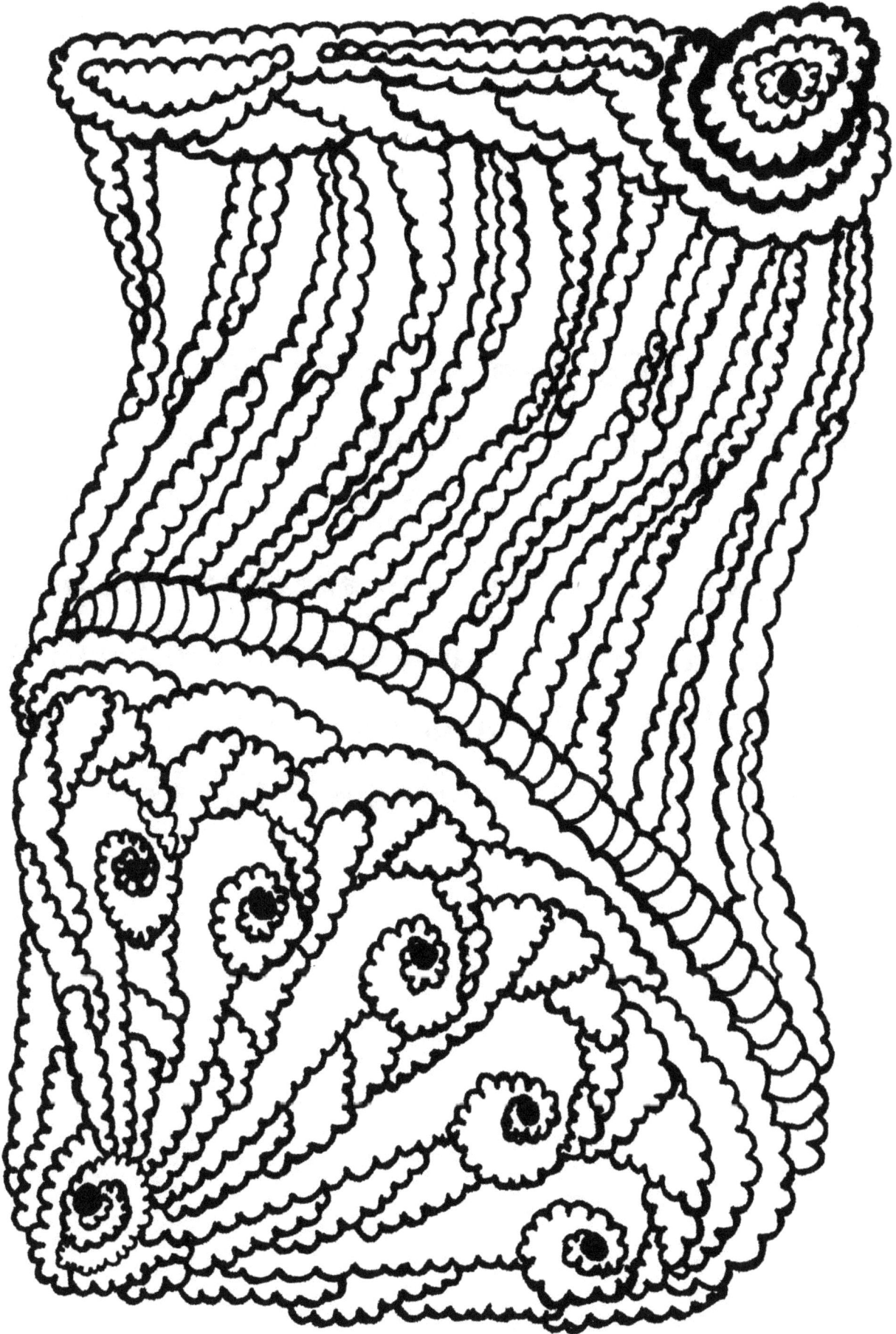

1 Corinthians 15:57-58

But thanks be to God, which giveth us the victory through our Lord Jesus Christ. Therefore, my beloved brethren, be ye steadfast, unmovable, always abounding in the work of the Lord, forasmuch as ye know that your labor is not in vain in the Lord.

Galatians 2:20

I am crucified with Christ: nevertheless, I live; yet not I, but Christ lives in me: and the life which I now live in the flesh I live by the faith of the Son of God, who loved me, and gave himself for me.

Proverbs 1:7
The fear of the Lord is the beginning of knowledge: but fools despise wisdom and instruction.

1 Peter 5:6

Humble yourselves therefore under the mighty hand of God, that he may exalt you in due time:

Isaiah 12:2

Behold, God is my salvation; I will trust, and not be afraid: for the Lord Jehovah is my strength and my song; he also is become my salvation.

Philippians 4:6-7

Be careful for nothing; but in everything by prayer and supplication with thanksgiving let your requests be made known unto God. And the peace of God, which passeth all understanding, shall keep your hearts and minds through Christ Jesus.

Ecclesiastes 3:14

I know that, whatsoever God doeth, it shall be forever: nothing can be put to it, nor any thing taken from it: and God doeth it, that men should fear before him.

Hebrews 11:1
Now faith is the substance of things hoped for,
the evidence of things not seen.

Romans 12:1-2

I beseech you therefore, brethren, by the mercies of God, that ye present your bodies a living sacrifice, holy, acceptable unto God, which is your reasonable service.

And be not conformed to this world: but be ye transformed by the renewing of your mind, that ye may prove what is that good, and acceptable, and perfect, will of God.

Mark 8:38

Whosoever therefore shall be ashamed of me and of my words in this adulterous and sinful generation; of him also shall the Son of man be ashamed, when he cometh in the glory of his Father with the holy angels.

Psalm 116:1-2

I love the LORD, because he hath heard my voice and my supplications.

Because he hath inclined his ear unto me, therefore will I call upon him as long as I live.

John 14:27
Peace I leave with you, my peace I give unto you: not as the world giveth, give I unto you. Let not your heart be troubled, neither let it be afraid.

Genesis 1:1
In the beginning God created the heaven and the earth.

1 John 4:8
He that loveth not knoweth not God; for God is love.

Psalm 145:21

My mouth shall speak the praise of the LORD: and let all flesh bless his holy name for ever and ever.

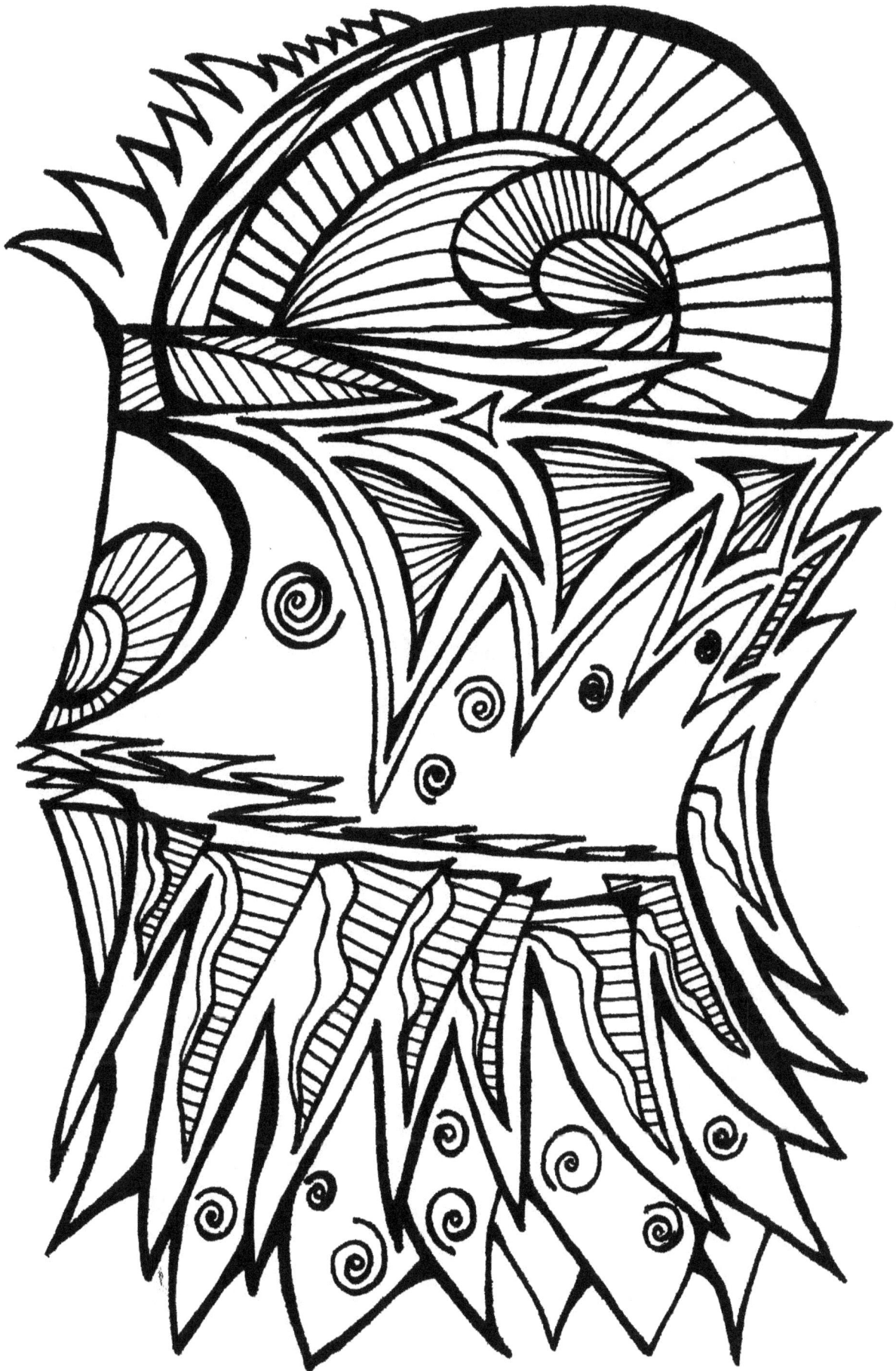

Nahum 1:7
The LORD is good, a strong hold in the day of trouble; and he knoweth them that trust in him.

Jeremiah 33:3
Call unto me, and I will answer thee, and show
thee great and mighty things, which thou
knowest not.

Romans 8:28
And we know that all things work together for good to them that love God, to them who are the called according to his purpose.

1 John 3:18

¹My little children, let us not love in word, neither in tongue; but in deed and in truth.

John 14:1
Let not your heart be troubled: ye believe in
God, believe also in me.

Psalm 145:21
My mouth shall speak the praise of the LORD: and let all flesh bless his holy name for ever and ever.

Philippians 1:6
Being confident of this very thing, that He which hath begun a good work in you will perform it until the day of Jesus Christ.

ABOUT THE AUTHOR

In 1977 Tanya Cochran was born in the beautiful state of Maine. Fresh from high school she became a floral designer and has loved her career choice for over 20 years. She has lived in 4 different states and has experienced many life changing events of which she is grateful mostly for the character they have built in her.

She is honored to be a wife (of 16yrs!) and mom of three amazing children! She has one teenager and one who is almost a teenager so that's two reasons for teenagers for having a special place in her heart which led to the coloring books being for teenagers. Tanya enjoys attending church with her family. Also with her family she enjoys, fun 1-2 day trips, campfires, board games, long walks in the Maine woods, swimming, reading, going out with the girls, and of course...ART!

Tanya truly loves all kinds of art. Some of her passions include, abstract drawing, Oil painting, wood carving, mixed media shadow boxes, sculpting, greeting cards, sewing elaborate doll dresses, and floral design. Tanya vows to never stop creating new things! Albert Einstein said, "True art is characterized by an Irresistible urge in the creative artist." Tanya completely agrees!

Tanya says concerning the books she has for sale: "I find drawing abstract art as in these books (Dip Me In Color) to be relaxing. It gives me a different kind of comforting joy. I hope you feel that joy as you color the pages. Art is something that the creative person must get out and it's an honor to be able to share what's in my imagination with you! God certainly gave me a quirky mind and I'm grateful!

Thanks again for all your support! Hugs!

Scripture List... Book 2

Psalm 23:4

Psalm 89:11

Matthew 7:7

Psalm 16:8

1 Corinthians 13:13

Psalm 46:10

Proverbs 3:5-6

Isaiah 40:31

John 8:32

Philippians 1:6

Matthew 25:40

Psalm 19:14

John 16:33

2 Timothy 2:7

Matthew 11:28-30

Matthew 6:19-21

Psalm 88:2

1 John 3:18

Revelation 1:8

Proverbs 30:5

Psalm 119:11

Psalm 31:24

Jeremiah 33:3

Nahum 1:7

Psalm 145:21

Micah 6:8

Jeremiah 32:27

Isaiah 55:12

1 Corinthians 15:57-58

Galatians 2:20

Proverbs 1:7

1 Peter 5:6

Isaiah 12:2

Philippians 4:6-7

Ecclesiastes 3:14

Hebrews 11:1

Romans 12:1-2

Mark 8:38

Psalm 116:1-2

John 14:27

Genesis 1:1

1 John 4:8

Psalm 145:21

Nahum 1:7

Jeremiah 33:3

Romans 8:28

1 John 3:18

John 14:1

Psalm 36:5

Philippians 1:6